STAYING MENTALLY HEALTHY

Other Books in the LIVING PROUD! Series

Being Transgender

Coming Out and Seeking Support

Confronting Stereotypes

Engaging with Politics

Facing Homophobia

Finding Community

Keeping Physically Healthy

Living with Religion and Faith

Understanding Sexual Orientation and Gender Identity

LIVING PROUD! GROWING UP LGBTQ

STAYING MENTALLY HEALTHY

Robert Rodi and Laura Ross

Foreword by Kevin Jennings
Founder, GLSEN (the Gay, Lesbian & Straight
Education Network)

MASON CREST

Mason Crest
450 Parkway Drive, Suite D
Broomall, PA 19008
www.masoncrest.com

Printed in the United States of America

First printing
9 8 7 6 5 4 3 2 1

Series ISBN: 978-1-4222-3501-0
Hardcover ISBN: 978-1-4222-3510-2
ebook ISBN: 978-1-4222-8383-7

Cataloging-in-Publication Data is available on file at the Library of Congress.

Developed and Produced by Print Matters Productions, Inc. (www.printmattersinc.com)
Cover and Interior Design by Kris Tobiassen, Matchbook Digital

Picture credits: 10, Gimini/ABACAUSA.COM/Newscom; 12, Anchiy/iStock; 14, Wikimedia Creative Commons; 16, Wikimedia Creative Commons; 20, Richard Gardner/REX/Newscom; 25, Monkey Business/Fotolia; 27, Todor Tsvetkov/iStock; 30, gemenacom/iStock; 33, P_Wei/iStock; 36, De Visu/ Shutterstock; 42, Christopher Futcher/iStock; 45, Phase4 Photography/Fotolia; 47, GCShutter/iStock; 51, Hailshadow/iStock; 54, Yalayama/Fotalia; 61, Feverpitched/iStock
Front cover: nikoniko_happy/iStock

STAYING MENTALLY HEALTHY

CONTENTS

KEY ICONS TO LOOK FOR

Text-Dependent Questions: These questions send the reader back to the text for more careful attention to the evidence presented there.

Words to Understand: These words with their easy-to-understand definitions will increase the reader's understanding of the text while building vocabulary skills.

Series Glossary of Key Terms: This back-of-the-book glossary contains terminology used throughout this series. Words found here increase the reader's ability to read and comprehend higher-level books and articles in this field.

Research Projects: Readers are pointed toward areas of further inquiry connected to each chapter. Suggestions are provided for projects that encourage deeper research and analysis.

Sidebars: This boxed material within the main text allows readers to build knowledge, gain insights, explore possibilities, and broaden their perspectives by weaving together additional information to provide realistic and holistic perspectives.

FOREWORD

I loved libraries as a kid.

Every Saturday my mom and I would drive from the trailer where we lived on an unpaved road in the unincorporated town of Lewisville, North Carolina, and make the long drive to the "big city" of Winston-Salem to go to the downtown public library, where I would spend joyous hours perusing books on the shelves. I'd end up lugging home as many books as my arms could carry and generally would devour them over the next seven days, all the while eagerly anticipating next week's trip. The library opened up all kinds of worlds to me—all kinds of worlds, except a gay one.

Oh, I found some "gay" books, even in the dark days of the 1970s. I'm not sure how I did, but I found my way to authors like Tennessee Williams, Yukio Mishima, and Gore Vidal. While these great artists created masterpieces of literature that affirmed that there were indeed other gay people in the universe, their portrayals of often-doomed gay men hardly made me feel hopeful about my future. It was better than nothing, but not much better. I felt so lonely and isolated I attempted to take my own life my junior year of high school.

In the 35 years since I graduated from high school in 1981, much has changed. Gay–straight alliances (an idea my students and I pioneered at Concord Academy in 1988) are now widespread in American schools. Out LGBT (lesbian, gay, bisexual, and transgender) celebrities and programs with LGBT themes are commonplace on the airwaves. Oregon has a proud bisexual governor, multiple members of Congress are out as lesbian, gay, or bisexual, and the White House was bathed in rainbow colors the day marriage equality became the law of the land in 2015. It gets better, indeed.

So why do we need the Living Proud! series?

- Because GLSEN (the Gay, Lesbian & Straight Education Network) reports that over two-thirds of LGBT students routinely hear anti-LGBT language at school.

- Because GLSEN reports that over 60% of LGBT students do not feel safe at school.
- Because the CDC (the Centers for Disease Control and Prevention, a U.S. government agency) reports that lesbian and gay students are four times more likely to attempt suicide than heterosexual students

In my current role as the executive director of the Arcus Foundation (the world's largest financial supporter of LGBT rights), I work in dozens of countries and see how far there still is to go. In over 70 countries same-sex relations are crimes under existing laws: in 8, they are a crime punishable by the death penalty. It's better, but it's not all better—especially in our libraries, where there remains a need for books that address LGBT issues that are appropriate for young people, books that will erase both the sense of isolation so many young LGBT people still feel as well as the ignorance so many non-LGBT young people have, ignorance that leads to the hate and violence that still plagues our community, both at home and abroad.

The Living Proud! series will change that and will save lives. By providing accurate, age-appropriate information to young people of all sexual orientations and gender identities, the Living Proud! series will help young people understand the complexities of the LGBT experience. Young LGBT people will see themselves in its pages, and that reflection will help them see a future full of hope and promise. I wish Living Proud! had been on the shelves of the Winston-Salem/Forsyth County Public Library back in the seventies. It would have changed my life. I'm confident that it will have as big an impact on its readers today as it would have had on me back then. And I commend it to readers of any age.

Kevin Jennings
Founder, GLSEN (the Gay, Lesbian & Straight Education Network)
Executive Director, Arcus Foundation

GLSEN®

GLSEN is the leading national education organization focused on ensuring safe and affirming schools for all students. GLSEN seeks to develop school climates where difference is valued for the positive contribution it makes to creating a more vibrant and diverse community.
www.glsen.org

Dan Savage (right) and his husband Terry Miller received a special Emmy Award for their It Gets Better Project. The website www.itgetsbetter.org features more than 50,000 inspiring videos, many from celebrities, talking about coming out, overcoming bullying, and creating a life worth living.

STAYING MENTALLY HEALTHY

There are millions of LGBT people leading happy, healthy, and productive lives.

1

"AM I NORMAL?"

 WORDS TO UNDERSTAND

LGBT: Short for lesbian, gay, bisexual, and transgender, and considered to be more inclusive than just saying "gay." (Sometimes a Q is added at the end to represent *questioning* or *queer*.

Discrimination: Treatment of people as different because of a certain characteristic about them, such as race, religion, gender identity, or sexual orientation.

Harassment: When someone is continually bothered or tormented by another.

Homosexuality and gender nonconformity have existed in various cultures around the globe for centuries. Despite many efforts to erase LGBT lives and suppress all evidence of their existence we are today more aware than ever of the debt our civilization owes to LGBT individuals.

And yet everyone who experiences same-sex attraction or who identifies as transgender still wonders the same thing at some point in his or her life:

"Am I normal?"

There is no simple answer to this question because "normal" is an extremely difficult word to define. Likewise, the ways in which same-sex attraction and gender identity have been regarded over the course of history have dramatically changed—and continue to evolve.

Historical Views on Homosexuality

In the eleventh century, Saint Peter Damien introduced the term *sodomy*. It was taken from the biblical story of Sodom, where the sinful behavior of the inhabitants led to the destruction of the city. The word became commonly used to refer to a particular type of sexual intercourse between two men. In Europe, and later in America, sodomy was considered a crime based on biblical law.

In the 1800s, German lawyer Karl Heinrich Ulrichs was one of the first to speak out on behalf of LGBT people.

Medical and scientific issues related to homosexuality became more widespread in the nineteenth century, when German lawyer Karl Heinrich Ulrichs argued that homosexuality was an inherited biological condition and not a matter of immorality. He was one of the first pioneers of gay civil rights, fighting against anti-sodomy laws in the late 1800s. Around that time, the word *homosexual* was introduced.

Sigmund Freud, considered the father of psychoanalysis, studied homo-sexuality at the beginning of the twentieth century. In the course of his research, he came to believe that homosexuality could be a natural outcome of normal development. But after Freud's death, other researchers considered

 CLOSE-UP: SIGMUND FREUD IN DEFENSE OF HOMOSEXUALS

After a lot of study and thought, Freud determined that all human beings started out life as bisexual, then became either heterosexual or homo-sexual as a result of their experiences with parents and others. Unlike his colleagues and most people of his time, he did not view homosexu-ality as a form of mental illness, but simply as a normal human option. In a now-famous letter to an American mother in 1935, he wrote:

his theories flawed, and most medical professionals believed that only het-erosexuality was "normal." Homosexuality was considered a mental illness.

Homosexuality is assuredly no advantage, but it is nothing to be ashamed of, no vice, no degradation, it cannot be classified as an llness. . . . Many highly respectable individuals of ancient and modern times have been homosexuals, several of the greatest men among them (Plato, Michelangelo, Leonardo da Vinci, etc.). It is a great injustice to persecute homosexuality as a crime, and cruelty, too.

Homosexuality as a "Mental Disorder"

When the American Psychiatric Association (APA) first published the *Diagnostic and Statistical Manual of Mental Disorders* (known as the *DSM*) in 1952, it listed homosexuality as a mental disorder. The *DSM*, which is still published today but has been revised a number of times since that first edition, is meant to serve as a tool to guide general psychiatric study, research, and treatment—but it tends to reflect the mainstream cultural attitudes of its time.

The psychological concepts behind theories of mental disorders are very complicated and, as happens with all science, new information and technology can provide new answers. Beginning in the 1940s, research

ALFRED KINSEY
Reflections in the mirror of Venus.

In 1953, *Time* magazine horded Alfred Kinsey for his groundbreaking work on human sexuality. Thanks to Kinsey, people began to understand that homosexuality and bisexuality were not mental disorders.

on sexuality and mental health by Dr. Alfred Kinsey and psychologist Evelyn Hooker resulted in mounting evidence that homosexuality was *not* a mental disorder.

By the time the second edition of the *DSM* (known as *DSM-II*) was published in 1968, homosexuality was listed as a "sexual deviation," as opposed to a personality disturbance. Researchers were starting to take a broader view, but there was still a lot to learn.

 CLOSE-UP: TRANSGENDER IDENTITY AND THE *DSM*

DSM-IV used the term *gender identity disorder* to identify a set of experiences sometimes seen in transgender individuals. In its latest update, *DSM V*, gender identity disorder was reclassified as *gender dysphoria* and listed under a new category, distinct from sexual disorders. This diagnosis does not apply to all transgender people; it is only considered when an individual requires treatment to deal with significant discontent related to their gender identity. Nonetheless, there are many experts who believe that gender dysphoria should not be classified in the *DSM* at all, as it serves to reinforce notions that being transgender is a disorder.

The following year, when a police raid on a gay bar prompted the historic Stonewall Riots in New York, the movement for gay civil rights picked up steam. **LGBT** activists began to speak out against the attitude of the APA, and specifically the presence of homosexuality in the *DSM* at all, regardless of its classification. In 1973, the APA removed homosexuality from its list of mental disorders, and numerous other major medical organizations did the same.

Since then, the APA has attempted to reverse some of the negative effects that the original *DSM* classification had on homosexual people. The organization has opposed employment **discrimination** based on sexual orientation, the dismissal of gay and lesbian people from the military, and medical treatments designed to "cure" someone of homosexuality.

Victimized by Culture, Not Nature

As has been true for centuries, the influence of the Bible and other religious texts and beliefs continues to lead some people to consider homosexuality immoral or sinful. Some claim that increased instances of mental health problems such as depression or substance abuse are more common in the LGBT community as a result of engaging in behavior that is wrong and harmful. Nonetheless, most scientific experts today agree that being gay is not an illness or a mental disorder, but simply a natural occurrence in human sexual development.

So, why do LGBT people tend to suffer from depression and other problems more often than their straight counterparts do? The logical answer is that it is due to outside forces. When someone is subjected to **harassment** or abuse, rejection by friends and family, or even just painful self-doubt, it's only natural that he or she might get depressed, and even turn to drugs or alcohol to try to feel better.

"We tell people to think of it in terms of ice-cream preferences," says Adrienne Hudek, a community educator on LGBT issues. "You like strawberry ice cream, but everyone else likes vanilla. And because of that, people are mean to you and make fun of you. They treat you badly, and maybe they even hurt you. Naturally, this is very upsetting to you. You get so upset, you need treatment from a mental health professional. Does that mean you were sick because you liked strawberry ice cream in the first place? Of course not. You became sick because of what the other people did to you, not because of who you are."

There's no question that significant mental health issues affect the LGBT community. Many do suffer from depression, substance abuse, and poor general health. Too many attempt suicide.

Comments Hudek, "This is an important distinction to make, because people look at the statistics and say, 'Wow, a lot of gay people are depressed or commit suicide. That just proves they were sick to begin with or that they shouldn't be gay.' But that's not the case at all. There are millions of gay and lesbian people out there leading happy, healthy, and productive lives. But there are also some people who need a little bit of help to get there, and that's where mental health treatment comes in. There's absolutely nothing to be ashamed of, and there's no reason to be afraid of help when you need it."

 TEXT-DEPENDENT QUESTIONS

- What is the basis for the religious objection to homosexuality?
- What was the basis for the original psychiatric evaluation of homosexuality as a mental illness?
- What outside influences are the principle causes of emotional challenges for LGBT people?

 RESEARCH PROJECTS

- Define what, in your community, is considered "normal."
- Read some online essays or articles about psychiatry's evolving view of homosexuality during the past century.
- In your own words, describe the difference between "sexual disorder," "sexual deviation," and "sexual orientation."

Country singer Chely Wright has spoken out on behalf of LGBT young people who are facing suicidal thoughts as she once did.

2

DEPRESSION AND SUICIDE

 WORDS TO UNDERSTAND

Trauma: A deeply disturbing or distressing experience.
Pediatrics: The branch of medicine dealing with children and their diseases.
Quackery: When an untrained person gives medical advice or treatment, pretending to be a doctor or other medical expert.
Malpractice: When a doctor or other professional gives bad advice or treatment, either because of ignorance, negligence, or on purpose.

When country singer Chely Wright was sixteen, she knew she was a lesbian. She was mostly comfortable with her identity inside, but she believed she could never show it on the outside.

"For the most part, I knew, I guess I'm okay," she says. "But I also knew—you have to hide this because I'm either going to get the crap beaten out of me, or I'm going to get in big trouble. And I know I'm not going to fit in school. I know I'm not going to make it to the stage of the [Grand Ole] Opry. My band's not going to get hired. My dreams of country music wouldn't pan out."

As her career progressed, she had public relationships with men and kept her gay life hidden. For years, she struggled with trying to find happiness when she had to deny such an important part of herself. Even though she had commercial success, earning an Academy of Country Music Award and nominations for three Country Music Association Awards, she was depressed about the piece of her life that was missing.

Then, when she was in her mid-thirties, she found herself standing in her home, staring at herself in the mirror. She had a gun in her mouth, and she was ready to pull the trigger.

Driven Toward Self-destruction

"At that moment," Chely says, "I was looking at myself and feeling like I was outside of my body, watching somebody do something that I had made such a harsh judgment about my entire life. I had been so critical of people who had committed suicide; I judged them for being godless and weak. And I was watching that in the mirror and realizing, 'Holy crap! That's me.'

"But as I was about to pull the trigger, I realized I wasn't crying. And I was shocked: Shouldn't I be crying? Don't people cry when they kill themselves? Isn't it supposed to be more emotional than this?

"And as I was about to pull my thumb back and do it, I said a prayer to God to forgive me for what I was about to do because I know the gift of life is the most precious thing. And I had some things in my life that kind of flashed through my brain, and one of them was sunlight, and I thought about my dogs, and I thought about music and how much I love music. And I thought about a kiss from my partner, my ex-partner—the only love in my life I'd ever known—and I heard a noise, and it was the sound of my heart pounding in my head.

"And I looked up in the mirror again, and my eyes were just welled up with tears, and my cheeks were wet, and tears were streaming down. I could barely even see. I couldn't focus because there were so many tears coming out of my eyes. And the dam broke. And my emotions enveloped me, and I became one with myself again. I got back into my body. I was

 CLOSE-UP: "IT GETS BETTER"

Several years ago, gay advice columnist Dan Savage created a YouTube video with his partner, Terry Miller, to reassure LGBT youth who were dealing with harassment and persecution that their lives would improve as they got older. Other people, inspired by Savage and Miller, added their own videos, and suddenly a movement was born—a movement directly aimed at reducing LGBT suicides and inspiring hope in young LGBT people everywhere.

The It Gets Better Project is now a worldwide movement, with more than 50,000 user-created videos that have been viewed more than 50 million times! People offering their own stories and inspiration include everyday LGBT people who have found happiness and fulfillment in adulthood, as well as such prominent LGBT celebrities as Adam Lambert, Tim Gunn, Ellen DeGeneres, and Suze Orman. There are even videos by high-profile straight allies ranging from Sarah Silverman to President Obama.

"ItGetsBetter.org is a place where young people who are lesbian, gay, bisexual, or transgender can see how love and happiness can be a reality in their future," the project's website declares. "It's a place where our straight allies can visit and support their friends and family members. It's a place where people can share their stories, take the It Gets Better Project pledge and watch videos of love and support."

no longer outside of my body watching this cold person—this human with a gun in her mouth. I didn't know that I wasn't going to—on the next day—kill myself. I knew on that night I wouldn't do it."

Wright was never tempted to take such a drastic action again, and instead she began to accept who she really was. She decided to come out publicly, a move that she believes set her free and gave her a personal and professional rebirth.

Feeling Overwhelmed and Oppressed

For thousands of LGBT people, suicide seems like the only option when they are faced with the immense struggles and stress of understanding and accepting their sexual orientation.

As part of the normal experience of growing up, many teenagers encounter significant feelings of stress, confusion, and self-doubt. These intense feelings can be overwhelming for anyone, which is why suicide is the third leading cause of death among young people ages fifteen to twenty-four. And these emotions are often much more challenging for LGBT youth, especially if they don't have the resources or support necessary to help them. Studies have shown that LGBT young people who do not receive support from their families are more than eight times as likely to attempt suicide than their peers who do have support.

Much research has been done to determine exactly why this is the case. The increased number of suicide attempts among LGBT people is not because of their sexual orientation itself. In other words, feeling suicidal

All teens experience times of depression and loneliness. But when feelings of sadness and isolation become overwhelming, you should seek help from a therapist or psychologist who understands the pressures LGBT people face.

is not part of being gay or the result of coming out. Instead, these feelings can come as a response to being bullied at school, being treated poorly at home or in a religious community, or feeling as if they have failed to live up to expectations of being "normal."

"Families and caregivers have a dramatic and compelling impact on their LGBT children's health, mental health, and well being," says Caitlin Ryan, director of the Family Acceptance Project, who works with parents of LGBT children. "We tell parents and families that they need to provide a supportive environment for their children before they know who they'll become."

Depression: A Treatable Illness

Being gay or lesbian isn't something individuals can control or change. So when LGBT people hear their friends or families make jokes about other gay people, it can have a strong and lasting impression. Likewise, when people exploring their own sexuality believe that others will not accept them if they know they are gay, they're more inclined to hide their feelings.

When anyone is told they are bad or wrong because of who they are, that **trauma** and stress can lead to mental health issues such as depression or anxiety. This is frequently what happens to LGBT people and others who are considered different from their peers, putting them at risk for suicide.

Depression is a medical condition. Individuals suffering from depression may constantly feel sad or tense.

"At first I was feeling sad all the time, even though I had no reason to be," says Rob, who shared his experience with depression on the resource website 4therapy.com. "Then the sadness turned into anger, and I started having fights with my family and friends. I felt really bad about myself, like I wasn't good enough for anyone. It got so bad that I wished I would go to bed and never wake up."

People struggling with depression often lose energy and feel restless or tired all the time. In some cases, this can lead to thinking that suicide is the only way out of feeling bad, or the only way to fix a very difficult situation.

"Teens need to know that they can go to their parents with a problem and their parents won't hate them or hit them and they could talk it through," says Ryan.

Parents, family members, and friends also need to be able to recognize the signs of depression. In Rob's case, his brother noticed that his behavior changed and immediately suggested that Rob see a doctor. Rob did, and he learned that depression is a real illness. It's not something that can be fixed by being told to "cheer up" and be happy. Like all medical problems, the most effective treatment will come from a doctor or other healthcare professional. Rob began seeing a therapist regularly, who helped him talk through his problems.

"This treatment helps me control depression in my everyday life," he says. "It has taken some time, but I'm finally feeling like myself again."

Alcohol may temporarily dull the pain, but in the long run, it makes people who are depressed feel even worse.

Alcohol Abuse, Isolation, and Other Danger Signs

People who don't understand that depression is an illness often seek cures or treatments that may seem to work in the short term by dulling the pain—such as drugs or alcohol—but these things don't get to the root of the problem and can lead to addiction, which is a huge problem in itself. In fact, alcohol is a depressant; in the long run, it just makes people who are depressed feel even worse.

In a similar way, when parents, friends, and other family members don't understand what it means to be LGBT, they often look for some type of treatment or "cure"—something that can turn a gay person straight. While people may be able to change the way they behave, experts explain that a person's identity on the inside isn't something that can be altered or made different. And often, attempting to do this does much more harm than good.

"If kids get the message that who they are is unacceptable, then they will carry that scar for the rest of their lives," says Gary Remafedi, a professor of **pediatrics** at the University of Minnesota. "Telling parents that [homosexuality] is an illness, that they should force their children to seek some cure that doesn't exist, is **quackery** and it's **malpractice**."

All of this can also increase feelings of depression and isolation. When people reach the point of feeling hopeless enough to consider suicide, there are often outward signs and indicators. They may see themselves as bad or inferior people and tell their friends about those feelings. Suicidal teens may also withdraw from their friends, spend time alone, abuse drugs and alcohol, and lose interest in things they usually enjoy.

If you hear someone say that he or she is considering suicide, listen hard, take the person seriously, and encourage conversation about it.

Sometimes just talking about the issues—whether with a parent, friend, or mental health professional—can be very helpful. The key when someone you care about is in a desperate state of mind—or when you are—is to not ignore these feelings and to seek help as soon as possible.

"Suicide is truly a permanent solution to a temporary problem," says Ashley Albright, who works for a suicide prevention program. "Although we can give you the number of completed and attempted suicides throughout the past decade, there is no way we can give how many times someone took the opportunity to listen, care—and a life was saved."

 ## TEXT-DEPENDENT QUESTIONS

- Why do some LGBT people feel that suicide is their only option?

- What are some of the signs that someone may be at risk for suicide?

- Is depression a psychological, emotional, or medical issue?

 ## RESEARCH PROJECTS

- Consider what you might say to a friend who you suspect is clinically depressed.

- Consider what you might say to a friend who you suspect may be contemplating suicide.

- Go to the "It Gets Better" website (itgetsbetter.org), and watch some of the testimonial videos.

Schools should be safe spaces for people of all gender identities and sexual orientations.

3

SELF-ESTEEM

 WORDS TO UNDERSTAND

Homophobic: Showing fear or hatred of homosexuals.
Demonize: Portray something or someone as evil.
Prevalent: Extremely common.
Stigmatize: Characterize as shameful and disgraceful.
Vulnerability: Openness to attack and capability of being hurt.

When Anna Rangos walked down the halls of her high school, she frequently heard **homophobic** slurs from her classmates. Eventually, it became so bad that she brought the issue to her district's school board.

"My self-esteem just totally dropped because of what was being said," she declares. "Every single year, there's an incident, and I've never seen a kid punished. After a while, it's so frustrating, it hurts a lot to have people say those things to you while not having people who are supposed to protect you do that."

In most American high schools, bullying isn't limited to lesbian, gay, bisexual, and transgender students. According to the National Center for Educational Statistics, about one in every three students between the ages of twelve and eighteen reported being bullied in school in 2009. Eight years earlier, only 14 percent of that population said they had experienced bullying.

But for LGBT students, this type of harassment can be even more damaging because it reinforces feelings of confusion or loneliness they may already have because they feel they are different from most of their classmates.

"That's So Gay"

Bullying has been cited as a probable contributor to many teen suicides, including high-profile cases involving students as young as eleven years old. This has led to a heightened awareness on the part of educators and parents of the effects of bullying.

"This is going to give a whole new complexion to bullying and prevention here in the United States," says Marlene Snyder, director of development for an anti-bullying program used in many American high schools. "The message that needs to get out is you need to pay attention to what the kids are doing, and there are programs out there that can help."

At Rangos's high school, there is a Gay-Straight Alliance. But she reports that not many of her classmates were willing to participate in the group because they were afraid of being labeled and harassed by other students. And it's not just out-and-out bullying that has an impact; thoughtless language can sting, too. When Rangos listened to the way

Organizations like GLSEN (the Gay, Lesbian & Straight Education Network) are working to eliminate bullying in schools.

other students in her school spoke, she often heard anti-gay statements that made her feel bad about herself, even when that wasn't the intention.

"When you use the phrase 'That's so gay,'" she says, "it may not seem harmful, but it still does hurt inside."

That phrase is often used as a slang way to say something is weird or strange—but the people using it should think more carefully about its true meaning and the impact it can have. What it implies is that being gay is wrong and negative, and hearing it used in this way can be very hurtful to an LGBT person.

LGBT Self-hatred

When a person begins to believe the insults and slurs thrown at him or her day after day, it can lead to something called internalized homophobia—when LGBT people think negatively about themselves and their lives. This often keeps LGBT people from coming out; instead of feeling proud of who they are, they feel the need to keep their sexual orientation a secret or even actively hide it.

"When I first got to Nashville . . . I worked at a theme park called Opryland, and there were gay boys in my cast," says gay country singer Chely Wright. "I don't know that there were any gay girls. But I was fully aware that I was gay, of course, and I was very sure that God was okay with me. Yet I slung daggers of hatred toward the gay boys because I was so afraid that they might identify something in me that would be some identifying factor—that they might be able to know that I was gay—and I wanted to throw them off in case they thought I might be."

That reaction is not at all uncommon, especially among people like Wright who have strong religious beliefs. She told the boys they were an abomination, and that what they did was disgusting. These were the messages that she had heard from her church and other people in her life.

As Wright got older and understood more about herself, she saw that this was wrong, and came from her own internalized homophobia. She realized that she had been so frightened of what other people might think of her that she attacked other people who were *like* her. After she came out, she strongly regretted behaving like that.

"When I would go into Tower Records in Nashville, I was recognized by the young kids that worked at the record store," she says. "In fact, they would bring records or posters for me to sign. And I was a fan of k.d. lang's music. But when she came out, I wouldn't purchase a k.d. lang or Melissa Etheridge [another openly gay musician] record in Nashville because I was afraid for them to see me buying it. That comes with a great deal of shame for me to admit. I'm embarrassed to admit that—but that's how deep the fear and pain went."

The Coming-out Cure

When a fellow singer asked Wright directly if she was gay, she denied it. In that moment, she realized something in her life had to change. She didn't believe that being gay was a sin, but she believed that lying was. And for the first time, instead of just hiding who she was, she had clearly lied about it.

This helped her decide to come out to the world. She didn't want to be one of those people who say one thing in public but do something else in their private life. She recognized that same behavior in other high-profile people—particularly politicians and religious leaders who would publicly **demonize** the LGBT community while privately being gay themselves.

For LGBT people who hear constantly that they are somehow bad or abnormal, it is very hard to see who they really are.

"I felt it was really important for me to stand up and admit that because it *is* so **prevalent** in our culture, in American society," she says. "Because we've got people writing legislation and people in public office, people in powerful positions who have the chance and the opportunity to write policy who are signing paperwork that goes against the gay community, and they themselves are closeted. And I thought it was really important that I say, 'Pay attention to those who are the most vocal against gays and lesbians because I can tell you—those who spew the most venom, pay attention to that.' Because I did it."

Adapting to Abuse

While some people may lash out at those who are like them due to their own confusion and self-hatred, others may find themselves stuck in dangerous or abusive situations. A recent study by the University of California Los Angeles (UCLA) shows that 27.9 percent of gay and lesbian adults and 40.6 percent of bisexual adults report intimate partner violence—that is, violence committed by a husband, wife, boyfriend, girlfriend, or lover. The numbers for gay, lesbian, and bisexual people are significantly higher than for straight couples, of which only 16.7 percent report incidents of intimate partner violence.

This doesn't meant that LGBT people are more abusive than straight people. What it means is that LGBT people are more willing to put up with abusive relationships than straight people are. Often, this is because they lack the self-esteem they need to protect themselves. They just don't understand that they deserve better, or don't have the strength to leave.

"Gays, lesbians, and bisexuals still face discrimination on a number of fronts," says Dr. Elaine Zahnd, one of the lead researchers on the UCLA study. "Some heterosexuals seek to **stigmatize** and isolate gays, lesbians, and bisexuals. Stigma and social isolation may result in lower self-esteem and increase one's **vulnerability** to abuse."

Alcohol, Drugs, and Unsafe Sex

Zahnd's research team also found that nearly one in ten people who report violence in their relationships also engage in binge drinking.

This is most likely a way to cope with the abuse, which many people feel they deserve, because they think of themselves as being worthless or hopeless.

"Self-medication to deal with stigma and discrimination may result in risky alcohol or drug use," she says. "Both mental and emotional health problems and risky alcohol and drug use have been shown to be associated with violent victimization. [In the study,] about one-third of the violence was associated with substance use. It may be to mask the pain, or it may occur in situations where mutual fighting or battering takes place."

Substance abuse is a significant health issue in the LGBT community. Excessive use of alcohol and drugs can lead to poor decision making and risky behaviors, including unprotected sex. That can put people at risk of contracting sexually transmitted diseases, such as HIV, the virus that causes AIDS. When LGBT people feel sinful or worthless because of their gender identity or sexual orientation, they may not feel that it's important to take care of their health or protect themselves from sexually transmitted diseases. Plus, they may turn to drinking and drugs to numb their pain. Over time, it may take more alcohol or harder drugs to keep those feelings of self-hatred buried, and that is why some LGBT people become addicted to drugs and alcohol—it has nothing to do with being LGBT in and of itself!

Patterns of Self-sabotage

"It happens all the time, and it becomes so familiar that you can almost see it coming a mile away," says Adrienne Hudek, who works with

CLOSE-UP: SELF-ESTEEM AND HIV/AIDS

Lots of people all over the world—including in the United States—think that HIV/AIDS is a "gay disease." People who have HIV/AIDS are sometimes rejected and discriminated against; some have lost their jobs or been the victims of violence. The stigma attached to HIV/AIDS has kept many people from seeking HIV testing—or from being treated once they've received a diagnosis. This can turn a potentially manageable chronic disease into a death sentence.

"Living with HIV/AIDS can damage more than our immune systems," according to *POZ* magazine; "it can also have a devastating impact on our self-esteem. The stigma and discrimination that often accompany HIV can make us feel self-conscious, afraid, less worthy or even depressed." As we've seen, isolation can make such feelings more intense, while coming together with others who are in similar circumstances does the opposite. In *POZ*'s words, "A strong sense of our self-esteem is linked to our ability to disclose our HIV status, practice safer sex, and connect to and stay in care."

Organizations such as the Gay Men's Health Crisis (GHMC) offer an extended community "where people come together to share and receive support, kindness and understanding. Participation in this community comes with a responsibility to one another and a commitment to be compassionate and ensure each other's safety and well-being." Local and online support groups for people living with HIV and AIDS are also effective at restoring and maintaining mental health and encouraging physical health as well.

at-risk youth in the LGBT community. "A guy who's barely even out of the closet yet goes to a gay club, and maybe he tries drugs or alcohol. And for the first time in probably a very long time, he feels good. He feels happy. The drugs make him forget about everything that's challenging in his life. He doesn't feel bad about who he is anymore. So when he goes home, and mom or dad tells him he's a sinner, or when kids at school threaten him and call him names, he remembers how good the drugs felt. He thinks about how great that was, compared to how bad his real life is. So he wants to do them again, because it makes it easier to deal with the pain and shame that he feels every day. But it doesn't really work out that way."

Researchers at the Family Acceptance Project at San Francisco State University studied the impact of family rejection or acceptance on LGBT people. What they found was that the people who reported high levels of rejection from their families during adolescence were eight times more likely to have attempted suicide by age twenty-five. They were also nearly six times more likely to have serious issues with depression, and their risks of abusing drugs and contracting sexually transmitted diseases were three times higher than that of the overall population.

"That just shows how serious and damaging it can be when kids feel like they have nowhere to turn," Hudek says. "The most effective way to stop this is to let kids know that there is help available to them. It's never easy. And no matter how they make someone feel at the time, drugs and alcohol make this so much worse, not better."

TEXT-DEPENDENT QUESTIONS

- What is *internalized homophobia,* and what causes it?

- How does the bullying of LGBT people lead to drug and alcohol addiction, abusive relationships, and suicide?

- What is the best way for LGBT people to reclaim their sense of self-worth?

 RESEARCH PROJECTS

- Search for "gay suicide" on the Internet, and see how many recent stories come up.

- Pay attention to the conversations you and your friends have every day; make a note of anything that might be hurtful or harmful to others.

- Try to recall the times in your own life when name-calling or bullying affected you; remember how you felt and what it took to get over it.

It's important to know that you are not alone. The support of friends, family, and LGBT support organizations can make all the difference.

4
GETTING HELP

 WORDS TO UNDERSTAND

Anonymity: Being unknown, having no one know who you are.
Credible: Believable, reliable.
Impetus: Something that causes or starts an action.
Ministry: A religious group or organization that works to help others in
   a certain way.
Dichotomy: A division into two opposite and contradictory groups.

In 1994, Peggy Rajski and Randy Stone won an Academy Award for
their short film *Trevor,* the story of a gay thirteen-year-old boy who attempted to kill himself after being rejected by his loved ones. A few years
later, when the film was scheduled to be aired on television, Rajski and
Stone realized that some people watching it might be struggling with
the same issues. They thought it would be a good idea to provide some
information on suicide prevention resources for lesbian, gay, bisexual,
and transgender teenagers. So they began to look for telephone numbers
or other information about these services.

They couldn't find any.

Rajski and Stone were so disturbed by that discovery that they created the Trevor Project, a nonprofit organization that features a twenty-four-hour crisis and suicide prevention telephone helpline available to people who might have no place else to turn. Today, it also includes a website that provides information to help parents and educators support LGBT young people.

Though the Trevor Project was founded to provide resources for suicidal LGBT youth, it also provides information to help them deal with issues before they reach such an extreme point. The website features an "Ask Trevor" page, where visitors can post confidential questions about issues of sexual orientation and identity. Trained counselors then supply answers and assist with finding additional resources that might be helpful. Topics addressed include everything from coming out to relationships to figuring out whether or not you're gay. The site also features past letters from other visitors, along with their responses, and provides information for family and friends of LGBT youth who want to be supportive.

Support, Advice—and Anonymity

Issues of identity are challenging for everyone, and answering those questions isn't simple. In fact, it's impossible for anyone to define someone else's sexual orientation. It's a personal issue, and one that people must work through and understand on their own.

Talking with a counselor or therapist provides a safe place to talk about your private feelings.

"I've been asked so many times, 'How do I know if I'm gay?'" says Adrienne Hudek, who helps connect LGBT people with mental health resources and support groups. "People will list off a bunch of things they do or say or think. And then they ask if that makes them gay. But it's not that simple. It's not something somebody else can tell you or answer for you. You have to answer it for yourself. But there are people out there who can help."

The issue of personal sexual orientation can be especially confusing for someone trying to sort through it alone, Hudek says. And many young people are unwilling to discuss their sexual identity with someone else. While some of them may be worried about homophobia or rejection, others may just be embarrassed to discuss such a personal and sexual thing. That's why the confidentiality and **anonymity** of the Internet can be comforting to anyone questioning his or her sexual orientation.

"Plenty of people have questions, and they don't feel comfortable asking a stranger, whether it's a social worker, counselor, or doctor," Hudek says. "That makes sense, because these can be very personal conversations. So we recommend some excellent websites that give some terrific, **credible** information. And the good part of that is, you really see that you're not alone. People all over the world are asking the same questions and dealing with the same issues."

The Wide Range of Online Resources

In addition to the Trevor Project, other websites and online communities have sprung up that provide helpful information and insight,

The Internet offers teens a way to connect with others like themselves, anywhere, any time. Just use caution online.

including Empty Closets, PFLAG (formerly Parents and Friends of Lesbians and Gays), Shout Out Health, and many others. Answers and advice are increasingly available on general-information websites as well. Go Ask Alice! is a health question-and-answer service produced by Columbia University that covers a wide range of topics, such as acne, fertility, aromatherapy, fitness, tattoo safety, and much more. It also provides guidance on LGBT issues, such as how to identify one's own orientation. For example, a reader asked about her possible bisexual feelings and received this response:

*We are often called to label ourselves as purely sexually inclined one way or the other, either to be attracted to guys or to girls only, end of story. But in actuality, most people fall somewhere on a spectrum of attraction, fantasy, desire, and action with people of all genders. The curiosity your friend has sparked in you could be just that—same-gender wonderings—or it could be the **impetus** for discovering that you are bisexual, and may be attracted to other women in the future.*

The pioneering sex researcher Alfred Kinsey broke from popular thinking on sexuality in the 1950s, theorizing that bisexuality was in fact far more common than previously thought. Kinsey is perhaps most famous for his sexual-orientation scale, which represents exclusive heterosexuality with a zero and exclusive homosexuality with a six—bisexuality is regarded as an approximate three, when a person is equally attracted to or has had sexual experiences (including fantasies) with both men and women.

Most humans experience erotic desires, act on those desires, and have relationships in a social context. Kinsey's research showed that bisexuals had more sexual experiences with one gender or another depending on their social environment. In other words, factors that we might not think of as sexual per se, like political and social ties, can in fact influence those who we choose to be with and whether we identify ourselves as straight, gay, bi, queer, etc.

Answers to Budding Sexual-identity Questions

The development of sexual orientation occurs throughout youth and adolescence. Studies show that young people, gay or straight, first become aware of sexual attraction by about age twelve. As they develop, many experiment with sexual activity. According to the American Academy of Pediatrics, a survey of thirteen-to-nineteen-year-olds found that one in ten boys and one in seventeen girls report having at least one same-sex sexual experience; however, most studies estimate that only 2 to 7 percent of U.S. teens consider themselves lesbian, gay, or bisexual.

"By the time children are eleven, twelve, and thirteen, they have a very good sense that their sexual orientation may be different from the majority of their friends," says Ellen Perrin, a developmental-behavioral pediatrician at the Floating Hospital for Children at Tufts Medical Center in Boston. "There is no evidence that people could become gay because of external influences."

That's why talking about these issues can be so helpful. Other people have likely had the same experiences, questions and concerns. The Gay and Lesbian National Hotline provides trained peer counselors who can help young people discuss their feelings and questions in a productive, nonjudgmental way. While there isn't always an easy way for people to answer questions about themselves, these resources can help.

Guidance Through Religious Issues

Many people struggling with LGBT issues feel conflicted because of their religious beliefs. Some religions teach that being gay is a sin and that sinners won't be admitted to heaven. They may even cite passages from the Bible or other religious texts that supposedly support intolerance toward LGBT people. This makes it difficult for faithful gay people to accept and embrace their own sexual orientation. Many don't want to come out—or even be who they are—if it places them at odds with their spiritual values.

But there are millions of LGBT people around the world who remain devoted to their religions while accepting and loving themselves and their sexual orientation. There are several denominations in Judaism, including Progressive and Reform Judaism, that accept and welcome gay and lesbian members. DignityUSA is an organization for LGBT Catholics, and there are hundreds of other gay-inclusive churches and Christian organizations throughout the United States. There are also organizations devoted to LGBT Muslims.

Grammy-nominated Christian singer Jennifer Knapp attracted the attention of the Christian community when she came out publicly. Though some were upset and disappointed by her declaration, she also received a lot of support. Inclusive religious leaders are optimistic that as more role models emerge, people will recognize that it is possible to be both gay and committed to your faith.

"A lot of youth are suicidal over their realization of their own sexuality," says Justin Lee, executive director of the Gay Christian Network, a

Millions of devout LGBT people find comfort and support in churches, temples, mosques, and synagogues that welcome worshippers of all gender identities and sexual orientations.

nonprofit **ministry** in Raleigh, North Carolina. "The **dichotomy** will continue in the church, but with high-profile artists coming out, we'll see the church reevaluate how it addresses these issues."

Answers, Not Avoidance

Considering all of the reasons some people may have to be afraid of it, it's important to remember that simply ignoring the issue of sexual identity won't make it go away. When someone is questioning his or her sexual orientation, the healthiest thing to do is to seek information and answers.

Finding supportive family members, friends, or mental health professionals can help people feel safe and secure as they work through their questions. If that's not an option, then speaking with a trained hotline counselor can be the next-best alternative.

"No one can tell you if you're gay, lesbian, bisexual, or straight, and nobody ever should," says Adrienne Hudek. "The purpose of these services isn't to convince someone that they're gay. We know that's not even possible. What we do is provide a safe and confidential way for people to be able to talk about things they might otherwise keep hidden inside, where they can really do damage. We talk openly and honestly about how people feel, so they can make healthy choices that are right for them."

TEXT-DEPENDENT QUESTIONS

- How does someone know if he or she is gay?

- How does the anonymity of support websites and online communities help some LGBT people confront their problems?

- How can religion be a negative influence on LGBT believers' lives? How can it be a positive one?

 RESEARCH PROJECTS

- Check out the resources and services available at The Trevor Project (thetrevorproject.com).

- If there's an LGBT support group in your neighborhood, ask to sit in on a meeting.

- Join the Gay-Straight Alliance at your school; if there isn't one, consider starting one.

Self-image can be a fragile thing. Letting others label you will keep you from seeing yourself as the complete person you really are.

SERIES GLOSSARY

Activists: People committed to social change through political and personal action.

Advocacy: The process of supporting the rights of a group of people and speaking out on their behalf.

Alienation: A feeling of separation and distance from other people and from society.

Allies: People who support others in a cause.

Ambiguous: Something unclear or confusing.

Anonymous: Being unknown; having no one know who you are.

Assumption: A conclusion drawn without the benefit of real evidence.

Backlash: An adverse reaction by a large number of people, especially to a social or political development.

Bias: A tendency or preference toward a particular perspective or ideology that interferes with the ability to be impartial, unprejudiced, or objective.

Bigotry: Stubborn and complete intolerance of a religion, appearance, belief, or ethnic background that differs from one's own.

Binary: A system made up of two, and only two, parts.

Bohemian: Used to describe movements, people, or places characterized by nontraditional values and ways of life often coupled with an interest in the arts and political movements.

Caricature: An exaggerated representation of a person.

Celibate: Choosing not to have sex.

Chromosome: A microscopic thread of genes within a cell that carries all the information determining what a person is like, including his or her sex.

Cisgender: Someone who self-identifies with the gender he or she was assigned at birth.

Civil rights: The rights of a citizen to personal and political freedom under the law.

Clichés: Expressions that have become so overused—stereotypes, for example—that they tend to be used without thought.

Closeted: Choosing to conceal one's true sexual orientation or gender identity.

Compensating: Making up for something by trying harder or going further in the opposite direction.

Conservative: Cautious; resistant to change and new ideas.

Controversy: A disagreement, often involving a touchy subject about which differing opinions create tension and strong reactions.

Customs: Ideas and ways of doing things that are commonly understood and shared within a society.

Demonize: Portray something or someone as evil.

Denominations: Large groups of religious congregations united under a common faith and name, and organized under a single legal administration.

Derogatory: Critical or cruel, as in a term used to make a person feel devalued or humiliated.

Deviation: Something abnormal; something that has moved away from the standard.

Dichotomy: Division into two opposite and contradictory groups.

Discrimination: When someone is treated differently because of his or her race, sexual orientation, gender identity, religion, or some other factor.

Disproportionate: A situation where one particular group is overrepresented within a larger group.

Diverse: In the case of a community, one that is made up of people from many different backgrounds.

Effeminate: A word used to refer to men who have so-called feminine qualities.

Emasculated: Having had one's masculinity or manhood taken away.

Empathy: Feeling for another person; putting yourself mentally and emotionally in another person's place.

Empirical evidence: Factual data gathered from direct observation.

Empowering: Providing strength and energy; making someone feel powerful.

Endocrinologist: A medical doctor who specializes in the treatment of hormonal issues.

Epithets: Words or terms used in a derogatory way to put a person down.

The Establishment: The people who hold influence and power in society.

Extremist: Someone who is in favor of using extreme or radical measures, especially in politics and religion.

Flamboyant: Colorful and a bit outrageous.

Fundamentalist: Someone who believes in a particular religion's fundamental principles and follows them rigidly. When the word is used in connection with Christianity, it refers to a member of a form of Protestant Christianity that believes in the strict and literal interpretation of the Bible.

Gay liberation: The movement for the civil and legal rights of gay people that originated in the 1950s and emerged as a potent force for social and political change in the late 1960s and '70s.

Gender: A constructed sexual identity, whether masculine, feminine, or entirely different.

Gender identity: A person's self-image as female, male, or something entirely different, no matter what gender a person was assigned at birth.

Gender roles: Those activities and traits that are considered appropriate to males and females within a given culture.

Gene: A microscopic sequence of DNA located within a chromosome that determines a particular biological characteristic, such as eye color

Genitalia: The scientific term for the male and female sex organs.

Genocide: The large-scale murder and destruction of a particular group of people.

Grassroots: At a local level; usually used in reference to political action that begins within a community rather than on a national or global scale.

Harassed/harassment: Being teased, bullied, or physically threatened.

Hate crime: An illegal act in which the victim is targeted because of his or her race, religion, sexual orientation, or gender identity.

Homoerotic: Having to do with homosexual, or same-sex, love and desire.

Homophobia: The fear and hatred of homosexuality. A homophobic person is sometimes referred to as a "homophobe."

Horizontal hostility: Negative feeling among people within the same minority group.

Hormones: Chemicals produced by the body that regulate biological functions, including male and female gender traits, such as beard growth and breast development.

Identity: The way a person, or a group of people, defines and understands who they are.

Inborn: Traits, whether visible or not, that are a part of who we are at birth.

Inclusive: Open to all ideas and points of view.

Inhibitions: Feelings of guilt and shame that keep us from doing things we might otherwise want to do.

Internalized: Taken in; for example, when a person believes the negative opinions other people have of him, he has *internalized* their point of view and made it his own.

Interpretation: A particular way of understanding something.

Intervention: An organized effort to help people by changing their attitudes or behavior.

Karma: The force, recognized by both Hindus and Buddhists, that emanates from one's actions in this life; the concept that the good and bad things one does determine where he or she will end up in the next life.

Legitimized: Being taken seriously and having the support of large numbers of people.

LGBT: An initialism that stands for lesbian, gay, bisexual, and transgender. Sometimes a "Q" is added (**LGBTQ**) to include "questioning." "Q" may also stand for "queer."

Liberal: Open to new ideas; progressive; accepting and supportive of the ideas or identity of others.

Liberation: The act of being set free from oppression and persecution.

Mainstream: Accepted, understood, and supported by the majority of people.

Malpractice: When a doctor or other professional gives bad advice or treatment, either out of ignorance or deliberately.

Marginalize: Push someone to the sidelines, away from the rest of the world.

Mentor: Someone who teaches and offers support to another, often younger, person.

Monogamous: Having only one sexual or romantic partner.

Oppress: Keep another person or group of people in an inferior position.

Ostracized: Excluded from the rest of a group.

Out: For an LGBT person, the state of being open with other people about his or her sexual orientation or gender identity.

Outed: Revealed or exposed as LGBT against one's will.

Persona: A character or personality chosen by a person to change the way others perceive them.

Pioneers: People who are the first to try new things and experiment with new ways of life.

Politicized: Aware of one's rights and willing to demand them through political action.

Prejudice: An opinion (usually unfavorable) of a person or a group of people not based on actual knowledge.

Proactive: Taking action taken in advance of an anticipated situation or difficulty.

Progressive: Supporting human freedom and progress.

Psychologists and psychiatrists: Professionals who study the human mind and human behavior. Psychiatrists are medical doctors who can prescribe pills, whereas clinical psychologists provide talk therapy.

Quackery: When an untrained person gives medical advice or treatment, pretending to be a doctor or other medical expert.

The Right: In politics and religion, the side that is generally against social change and new ideas; often used interchangeably with *conservative*.

Segregation: Historically, a system of laws and customs that limited African Americans' access to many businesses, public spaces, schools, and neighborhoods that were "white only."

Sexual orientation: A person's physical and emotional attraction to the opposite sex (heterosexuality), the same sex (homosexuality), both sexes (bisexuality), or neither (asexuality).

Sociologists: People who study the way groups of humans behave.

Spectrum: A wide range of variations.

Stereotype: A caricature; a way to judge someone, probably unfairly, based on opinions you may have about a particular group they belong to.

Stigma: A mark of shame.

Subculture: A smaller group of people with similar interests and lifestyles within a larger group.

Taboo: Something that is forbidden.

Theories: Ideas or explanations based on research, experimentation, and evidence.

Tolerance: Acceptance of, and respect for, other people's differences.

Transgender: People who identify with a gender different from the one they were assigned at birth.

Transphobia: Fear or hatred of transgender people.

Variance: A range of differences within a category such as gender.

Victimized: Subjected to unfair and negative treatment, including violence, bullying, harassment, or prejudice.

A friend who accepts you for who you are can make all the difference.

FURTHER RESOURCES

GLBT National Help Center
Offering a national hotline, a national youth talkline, online peer-support chat, and other services.
www.glnh.org

The Trevor Project
Crisis intervention and suicide prevention services for LGBTQ people ages 13–24.
1-866-488-7386 • www.thetrevorproject.org

Gay, Lesbian, Bisexual and Transgender National Hotline
Provides telephone and online private one-to-one chat and email peer-support.
1-888-843-4564 • www.glbthotline.org/hotline.html

Live Out Loud
Inspiring and empowering LGBT youth by connecting them with successful LGBT professionals in their community.
www.liveoutloud.info

Empty Closets
A place "where you can figure out who you are, surrounded by other people just like you"—for LGBT people ages 13 and up.
www.emptyclosets.com

Go Ask Alice!
Advice from Columbia University health promotion specialists, healthcare providers, and more.
www.goaskalice.columbia.edu

Imaan
A British-based organization for LGBTQ Muslims.
www.imaan.org.uk

DignityUSA
Works for respect and justice for LGBT persons in the Catholic Church.
www.dignityusa.org

The World Congress of GLBT Jews/Keshet Ga'avah
Dedicated to creating a world where LGBT Jews can enjoy free and fulfilling lives.
www.glbtjews.org

INDEX